nature's
baby animals

BABY ANIMALS
OF THE DESERT

Carmen Bredeson

Dennis L. Claussen, Ph.D., *Series Science Consultant* Professor of Zoology, Miami University, Oxford, Ohio

Allan A. De Fina, Ph.D., *Series Literacy Consultant* Past President of the New Jersey Reading Association, Chairperson, Department of Literacy Education, New Jersey City University, Jersey City, New Jersey

CONTENTS

WORDS TO KNOW

burrow [BUR oh]—A hole in the ground where animals live.

den—The home of an animal in a cave or safe place.

endangered [ehn DAYN jurd] **animal**—A kind of animal that is in danger of disappearing from the earth forever.

WHERE ARE DESERTS?

= DESERTS

DESERTS

Deserts are very dry. Only a little bit of rain falls each year. It can get very hot in the desert. Many desert animals hide from the sun during the day. Baby animals have special ways to stay safe and live in the desert.

BABY KIT FOX

Baby kit foxes stay safe in a **den** when they are little. Kit foxes have very BIG ears. Big ears let out more heat from the fox's body than little ears would. Big ears help keep the foxes cool.

Sandgrouse babies are too little to go to a pond to drink. Their father can carry water in his belly feathers. He brings the water back to the nest. The thirsty chicks drink water right from the feathers.

Sandgrouse chicks can be hard to see!

BABY SANDGROUSE

BABY
AFRICAN DESERT ELEPHANT

A baby elephant is called a calf. Desert elephants can go for DAYS without drinking water! They also have very big feet for walking on soft sand.

The big hump
on a camel's back
is made of fat.
A camel uses the
fat for energy
when there is not
much food to eat.

A baby camel does not have a big hump.
It drinks milk from its mother. As the baby
grows, so does the hump.

This baby camel is one week old.

BABY
ARABIAN
CAMEL

BABY **MEERKAT**

Baby meerkats are called pups. They are born in cool **burrows** under the ground. Their mothers bring mice and lizards to the burrow. The pups learn to hunt by chasing the little animals.

Baby burrowing owls do not live in a nest. They are born in a burrow. Their parents bring mice, beetles, and birds for the chicks to eat. The chicks learn to fly when they are only six weeks old.

BABY

BURROWING OWL

BABY **GECKO**

Geckos are a kind of lizard. Baby geckos hatch from eggs. Desert geckos hide from the hot sun under rocks and plants. They hunt for insects and spiders at night when it is cooler.

Bighorn lambs have tiny horn buds when they are born. As the lambs grow, so do their horns. There are not many bighorn sheep left in the world. Many have been killed for their beautiful horns.

ENDANGERED ANIMAL OF THE DESERT

BABY

BIGHORN

SHEEP

Learn More

Books

Hickman, Pamela. *Animals and Their Young*. Tonawanda, N.Y.: Kids Can Press, 2003.

Lindeen, Carol. *Life in a Desert*. Mankato, Minn.: Capstone Press, 2004.

Ripple, William John. *Animals and Their Biomes—Desert Animals*. Mankato, Minn.: Capstone Press, 2005.

Sill, Cathryn. *About Habitats: Deserts*. Atlanta: Peachtree Press, 2007.

Missouri Botanical Garden

http://www.mbgnet.net

Click on Desert.

Enchanted Learning

http://www.enchantedlearning.com

Click on "Biomes." Then click on "Desert."

INDEX

~To our little Texans~Andrew, Charlie, and Kate~

Enslow Elementary, an imprint of Enslow Publishers, Inc.
Enslow Elementary® is a registered trademark of Enslow Publishers, Inc.

Library of Congress Cataloging-in-Publication Data

Bredeson, Carmen.
  Baby animals of the desert / Carmen Bredeson.
    p. cm. — (Nature's baby animals)
  Summary: "Up-close photos and information about baby animals of the desert biome"—Provided by publisher.
  Includes bibliographical references and index.
  ISBN-13: 978-0-7660-3007-7
  ISBN-10: 0-7660-3007-5
  1. Desert animals—Infancy—Juvenile literature. I. Title.
  QL116.B74 2008
  591.754—dc22
                        2007029287

Printed in the United States of America

10 9 8 7 6 5 4 3 2 1

Note to Parents and Teachers: The *Nature's Baby Animals* series supports the National Science Education Standards for K–4 science. The Words to Know section introduces subject-specific vocabulary words, including pronunciation and definitions. Early readers may need help with these new words.

To Our Readers: We have done our best to make sure all Internet addresses in this book were active and appropriate when we went to press. However, the author and the publisher have no control over and assume no liability for the material available on those Internet sites or on other Web sites they may link to. Any comments or suggestions can be sent by e-mail to comments@enslow.com or to the address on the back cover.

Every effort has been made to locate all copyright holders of material used in this book. If any errors or omissions have occurred, corrections will be made in future editions of this book.

♻ Enslow Publishers, Inc., is committed to printing our books on recycled paper. The paper in every book contains 10% to 30% post-consumer waste (PCW). The cover board on the outside of each book contains 100% PCW. Our goal is to do our part to help young people and the environment too!

Photo Credits: ardea.com: Thomas Dressler, p. 15; © 1999 Artville, LLC, p. 3; Corbis: Michael & Patricia Fogden, p. 9; Getty Images: Scott T. Smith, p. 6, Sean Russell, p. 20; Jean-Claude Carton/Bruce Coleman USA, p. 13; Minden Pictures: Bruce Davidson, p. 18, Gerry Ellis, p. 12, Yva Momatiuk & John Eastcott, p. 5, ZSSD, p. 21; naturepl.com: John Cancalosi, p. 7, Tom Vezo, p. 16, Tony Heald, pp. 10, 11, 23; NHPA: Ann & Steve Toon, pp. 2 (meerkat), 8, 14; Shutterstock, pp. 1, 2 (owls), 17; Visuals Unlimited: Jim Merli, p. 19.

Cover Photo: Shutterstock

Enslow Elementary
an imprint of
Enslow Publishers, Inc.
40 Industrial Road
Box 398
Berkeley Heights, NJ 07922
USA
http://www.enslow.com